From F ❀ *to Honey* ❀

The Story of Beekeeping

❀ by Joanne Mattern ❀

MODERN CURRICULUM PRESS
Pearson Learning Group

It is springtime. The meadows are alive with flowers. Suddenly you see a fuzzy, yellow and black creature flying from flower to flower. The creature flies right past some flowers. But it stops at others. After a few minutes, it zooms straight up. Then it is out of sight.

You've just seen a honeybee. What was it doing around those flowers? Where did it go? Why are bees so important to people?

Honeybees are creatures with unusual attributes. They are the only insects that produce a food that human beings eat. These amazing creatures live in large groups. There can be more than 50,000 bees in one group. Each bee has a special job.

People who take care of bees have a special job too. They are called beekeepers. They use special equipment to house the bees and collect the honey that bees make.

People have kept bees for thousands of years.
That is because the love of honey has persisted.
Today people use honey in all sorts of things—
from cakes to candy.

3

A bee's home is called a *hive*. Bees like to build hives in dark places. In the wild, a beehive might be in a hollow tree. Beekeepers build special containers to hold their bees.

Over the years, people have used many things to house bees. Some have used hollow logs and clay pots. Around 1500, beekeepers in Europe made upside-down basket hives called *skeps*.

There was always one big problem with keeping bees. They can be very aggressive when they are disturbed. Because of this attribute, a beekeeper had to kill the bees to get honey. Then, in 1851, an American named Lorenzo Langstroth invented the modern beehive. Langstroth built a hive out of wood that held movable frames. Each frame was covered with a sheet of wax called a *foundation*. These frames let beekeepers move bees. It also let them remove the honey without disturbing the bees. This type of hive also made it easy for beekeepers to enlarge the hive. All they had to do was add extra frames.

Inside the beehive is an amazing structure called a *honeycomb*. Honeycombs are made of thousands of six-sided wax cells. What is inside many of these cells? Yes, you guessed it. Honey! A honeycomb's cells tip upward. That way the honey does not drip out.

A honeycomb doesn't just hold honey. It also holds pollen for the bees to eat. And there are other cells, called *brood cells,* that hold eggs. These eggs may hatch into even more bees.

There are three different kinds of bees. Only the worker bees make honey. Worker bees are the smallest bees, and all of them are female. During their six-week lives, worker bees clean the hive, feed baby bees, build new wax cells, visit flowers, and make honey.

Another kind of bee is the drone. Drones are male. They live for about eight weeks. Their only job is to help produce offspring.

The queen bee is the largest bee in the hive. Each hive has only one queen. A queen can live as long as four years. Worker bees guard her, clean her, and feed her. The queen's only job is to lay eggs.

A special type of worker bee is called a field bee. It starts making honey by gathering nectar, a sweet liquid inside flowers. The worker collects nectar by sucking it with her tongue. She stores it in a special stomach. It is called a *honey sac*.

The field bee then flies back to the hive and passes the nectar to a house bee. The house bee places the nectar inside a honey cell. Later, other house bees cap the honey cell with a thin layer of wax. Inside the cell, the nectar dries out and becomes thicker. In a few weeks, it will turn into honey.

Beekeepers watch their hives carefully. They check to see that the bees are making many honey cells. They make sure their hives are placed near flowers that are full of nectar. They wrap the hives in plastic during the winter to keep the bees warm. In the summer, they move the hives into the shade to keep the bees cool. The summer months are the busiest times for beekeepers. That's when they collect the most honey.

Bees can be aggressive. So before a beekeeper can collect honey, the first thing he or she does is calm them. The beekeeper uses a tool called a *smoker* to blow smoke into the hive. Smoke makes the bees quiet and less likely to sting.

Beekeepers have other ways to keep from getting stung. They can wear clothes with elastic straps at the ankles and wrists. This way bees can't get up their sleeves or pant legs.

Beekeepers can also wear gloves and a special helmet to protect their faces. Beekeepers' clothes are usually white, because white calms bees.

Despite these precautions, beekeepers still get stung. Most of them have been stung so many times that they barely feel the sting.

When it is time to collect the honey, the beekeeper removes the frames from the hive. Then he or she uses a heated knife to scrape off the wax caps and open the honey cells. The frames are returned to the hive so the bees can refill them.

Then the beekeeper places the honeycomb in a special machine called an *extractor*. The extractor spins around and around until all the honey is out of the combs. Then the honey is strained to remove any bits of wax or dirt. Finally, the beekeeper pours the honey into jars. Now it's ready to eat!

Beekeepers don't collect honey late in the fall. That's because the bees eat honey during the winter, when there are no flowers to provide nectar. If a hive doesn't have enough honey for the winter, the beekeeper will put in sugar syrup to feed the bees. Otherwise, the bees could starve.

Running out of honey isn't the only problem a beekeeper faces. Bees can also *swarm*, or leave the hive. Bees often swarm when the hive gets too crowded. Then the queen bee and about half of the bees fly away and find a new place to live. The remaining bees will have a new queen, but not as many workers. That means the hive will produce less honey.

A beekeeper can tell when a hive is about to swarm. He or she can look at the hive to see if there are new cells with a baby queen in them. This can be a warning that the bees may be getting ready to swarm. If this happens, the beekeeper can add more frames to the hive. This gives the bees more room.

Honey is not the only product beekeepers get from hives. Bees also produce wax. Beeswax is used to make candles, cosmetics, and many other products.

Bees are also important to farmers. Beekeepers often rent their hives to farmers. Many plants need bees to carry pollen from flower to flower. This helps new plants to grow. Apples, pears, and melons are some foods that depend on bees.

Bees can be kept and used by people, but they are not pets. Bees in a commercial beehive are not tame animals. That is why beekeepers are careful when working around bees. They know they can be stung. So they take many steps to prevent that, such as using a smoker and wearing protective clothing.

Most of all, beekeepers respect their bees. They know that these insects must be treated with care. Beekeeping is a partnership that benefits both bees and people.

Fascinating Facts About Bees

- A worker bee can visit up to ten thousand flowers in a day, but all the nectar she collects during her life can only make about one teaspoon of honey.

- On a hot day, bees keep the inside of the hive cool by fanning their wings.

- A queen bee can lay as many as two thousand eggs a day—more than a million eggs in her lifetime.

- To make one pound of honey, bees must collect nectar from over a million flowers.

- Bees communicate by dancing! A bee's movements tell other bees how close flowers are to the hive. If the bee moves in a circle, the flowers are within a hundred yards. If she waggles her tail, they are farther away.